Love Calls Us Home

Daniel Free

Contents

Foreword

There is a profound wisdom, a soft whisper, and gentle loving Voice that can Divinely guide us throughout our days. All we have to do is take a moment to silence the world around us and go within. Daniel Free is a man who is deeply connected to the Holy Spirit and allows the Voice of the Holy Spirit to direct him. He is a bright light of love, truth, compassion, and understanding. He lives his life in integrity and honesty. The Voice of the Holy Spirit comes to Daniel, like a harmonious rhythm of beauty and truth. Through his poetry and messages, he clearly hears from the Holy Spirit. As you read Daniel's poetry you will feel the immense love and devotion that comes through him. You can feel the comfort and peace as you embrace the messages. There is only one truth, one God, one Voice, and you, like Daniel, can tune into it and live your life in peace and harmony, as Daniel does. I'm truly blessed and honored to know Daniel.

Sharon Lund, Author of
Sacred Living, Sacred Dying:
A Guide to Embracing Life and Death

Introduction

Solid Rock

This is time for Awakening, the Great Awakening of humanity. The world of illusions is a world of shifting sands, unstable, like a cloud blown with the wind. Our balance comes from God, our Rock. The imbalance of the world is apparent. It is not a firm foundation for God's Son. Our true foundation is the Presence of God, our stability, our stable dwelling place. We have lived on shifting sands for eons. God's Voice calls us Home.

Our Journey Home

God's Words alone,
no more to wait.
They bring us home
to Heaven's Gate.

To rest in God,
a quick advance.
No more to trod,
with God we dance.

Our journey home,
His holy place,
One with God,
no empty space.

He fills us all,
Heaven above.
We know His peace.
We know His Love.

Rocking Chair

A rocking chair,
a quiet place,
to sit with God,
to know His Grace.

To feel the love,
to see the trees,
to feel the wind,
to feel the breeze.

The waters flow,
a quiet stream,
a quiet life,
the grass so green.

We sit, we rest.
His peace now known.
We rest in God,
our holy Home.

His Love now here.
The grass so green,
the flowers bloom,
His Presence seen.

Listening

To hear God's Voice,
to receive His Word,
His Presence felt;
His Voice is heard.

To receive His gifts,
to hear God's Voice,
to know God's Love;
our hearts rejoice.

To open to Christ,
to receive His Word,
to feel God's Love;
His Voice now heard.

A new beginning,
A new day,
A holy life,
A holy way.

We rest in Him,
in God alone.
We have His Love.
We have come Home.

A New Day

I sit, I rest;
my mind at ease.
There is no quest—
my soul at peace.

Here with God,
a holy place,
the dawning light,
He fills the space.

The Love of God;
His Presence clear,
in Holy Silence
His Hand is here.

A quiet morning,
a new day born.
Home in God,
a new day dawns.

His Presence

Signs of His Presence,
Signs of His Love,
Sights and sounds
from Heaven above.

A world of miracles,
God's holy place.
A new world given
with God's Grace.

His Kingdom cometh.
The light is now clear.
All the darkness
does disappear.

The Light so bright,
no clouds in the sky,
no dark night,
to Heaven we fly.

We fly home.
Our souls are at peace.
We now rest
with grace and with ease.

Provisions

He opens our hearts to His Call for quiet, peace, and love. Provisions are made by Him Who knows our needs. Provisions from Providence. God provides. God provides all, is All, is in All.

A Morning Walk

A morning walk,
a quiet day,
a quiet street,
His holy way.

Morning light,
a quiet way,
a new day dawns,
a time to pray.

The green grass,
the hills, the trees;
a walk with God,
with love, with ease.

A new beginning,
a new day,
a new life,
a new way.

His Infinite Presence

His Infinite Presence,
the vast unknown.
All is given.
All is shown.

The Light of God
in every place.
The Love of God
in every face.

Every person,
every place,
now seen with love,
now seen with grace.

His Infinite Presence
now is known.
All is clear.
All is shown.

His Quiet Words

A quiet day,
His quiet words,
to know the truth;
His Voice now heard.

In the quiet,
in the grace,
His Holy Presence,
a holy place.

A place beyond,
Beyond the earth,
God's Holy Child,
a holy birth.

A holy place;
the love now seen.
With His Grace,
no hollow dream.

On hallowed ground,
where we now stand,
We bring peace
to all the land.

In the stillness,
God's quiet song.
In the silence
we are reborn.

We let go
and hear His words.
Deep in our hearts
His message heard.

A Picture Frame

A picture frame,
does reveal,
shows us God,
or does conceal.

A heavy frame,
filled with gold,
hides the truth;
the truth not told.

A heavy frame,
loud and bold,
does conceal
all that we hold.

A simple frame,
shining bright,
does reveal
God's Holy Light.

The Light of God;
we have our part,
the joy, the love,
in every heart.

The beauty seen.
The truth now told.
His quiet gifts,
what we now hold.

With God's Love

Awakening,
now at hand,
in each heart,
in every land.

Innocence;
we are now free.
With God's Love
we can now be.

All the travelling,
all the travail;
we are now home,
free from a jail.

Our Guiding Light,
a peaceful place,
filled with love,
filled with grace.

We see, we know;
the flowers bloom,
with God's Love,
in His room.

Here is Grace

Here is grace.
The past released.
All pain erased.
We have God's Peace.

The Peace of God
in every heart,
no longer hidden,
no more apart.

One with God;
we see the truth,
the call for love,
the answer soothes.

Soothes our souls,
heals us all.
We know love.
We hear God's Call.

God's Answer

Everything solved
with God's Hand.
All resolved,
His Holy Plan.

Problems big,
problems small;
God's Answer
solves them all.

One solution,
our release.
One Answer,
God's Peace.

No problems,
His Answer clear.
All solved,
His Presence here.

My Voice

My Voice here,
My Voice clear.
In quiet words
My Voice is heard.

In the Silence,
in the grace,
in the quiet;
a holy place.

The Peace of God
shining bright,
filled with love,
filled with light.

A holy place,
a place of rest,
our holy home,
we are so blessed.

Another Way

A path of safety,
a path of ease,
a path of joy,
the Way of Peace.

A rocky road,
with pebbles and stones,
leaves us empty,
all alone.

Which way
do we choose?
The Way of God,
or the blues?

We have wandered
for so long.
Sad and empty,
where we don't belong.

His Holy Kingdom
now awaits.
Do we choose for God,
or do we wait?

On barren soil,
we have gone,
not felt His Presence,
felt alone.

Felt the sadness
and the pain,
wandered alone,
in the rain.

We can go
another way.
A new beginning.
We choose today.

Into Christ's Presence
we enter now.
He shows the way.
He shows us how.

Tears of joy,
His Holy Place.
We know God's Love.
We know His Grace.

His Holy Place

Writing down,
the words so clear,
God is present,
God is here.

His holy place,
Home, we rest.
We have joy.
We are blessed.

In the quiet,
in the grace,
in the silence;
A holy space.

A new beginning,
His Presence here.
The Light of God
Shining clear.

Here

Here in all the pain,
Here the healing starts.
Here are all the blessings,
Here in every heart.

Here, a new beginning,
with your Holy Friend.
Here is a new world,
just around the bend.

A new world awaiting,
a place of love and ease.
God's Holy Kingdom,
filled with love and peace.

A holy place now given,
the Light, the Grace and more.
Here now we enter,
through an open door.

Here is His Holy Presence.
All the pain is shorn.
Here, a new beginning.
Here we are reborn.

God's Voice

Writing down
His Words, I hear.
All His Words,
His message clear.

God or the ego;
what voice do we choose?
His Song of love
or the blues?

On our decision
salvation rests.
His Holy Presence
or the ego's bequest?

Waking up
or wasting time?
He calls us Home.
Let freedom chime.

In truth,
there is only One Voice.
We are Home,
and we rejoice.

In truth,
there is no choice.
Only one voice is real,
and that's God's Voice.

Freedom's Gift

A world of boredom,
a world of pain;
illusions rule,
a world insane.

Nine to five,
by the clock.
No room to let
our souls rock.

Computers, tv,
the internet.
Where has all
the time been spent?

Where is God
in this place?
Our hearts, our souls
have been erased.

We can make
another choice.
We can awaken
and hear His Voice.

A new world,
not nine to five.
A new world
where we're alive.

No need for pills
or tv sets.
We are free
from the net.

We are Home.
With God we live.
Freedom's gift
is what He gives.

A place of joy,
with God's Grace.
A place of peace,
His Holy Place.

Rise

Rise from the ashes.
Rise from the grave.
Time to let go
of being a slave.

Relationships
that go nowhere,
not what God
would have us bear.

Specialness,
all the lies,
hidden in
a false disguise.

Seeking for love,
going outside,
we awaken
and open our eyes.

We awaken
and feel our hearts.
We feel God's Love,
the clouds depart.

A wake-up call,
we have God's Love.
A gift from Heaven,
from above.

No need to seek
or travel far.
All the love
is who we are.

All the love
we ever need
is in us all,
God's Holy Seed.

Holy relationships,
a solid base,
a firm foundation,
a Holy Place.

A place of love
where we can rest,
Amazing Grace,
we are so blessed.

Above the Earth,
there is no rift.
We have God's blessings.
We have God's gift.

Release

Choosing God.
Choosing peace.
Choosing now
to have release.

From the drama,
from the pain,
we awaken,
we are now sane.

A useless journey,
many trails,
filled with loss
and travails.

We now choose
another way,
a way of love,
a brand-new day.

We see the world
with new eyes,
all the love
that was disguised.

We have love.
We have peace.
We have joy.
We are released.

A new life
for us all,
as it was
before the fall.

A timeless journey,
A holy place,
All the pain
has been erased.

A new beginning.
A new way.
A new life
begins today.

Everything
falling into place.
All aligned
with God's Grace.

We now sail
to a new shore.
We have God's love
forever more.

We have love,
a holy place.
We have peace,
Amazing Grace.

Always There

His direction,
His plan,
Everything
in God's Hands.

He gives His gifts.
He gives His Love.
With His Grace
our lives unfold.

A gentle journey,
We come Home.
One with God;
we're not alone.

We are strong.
We are whole.
He fills our hearts.
He fills our souls.

In God we trust.
We now let go,
We have faith.
We see, we know.

We are enfolded
in His Care.
He is with us,
always there.

Walking in the Silence

We can walk in the Silence.
We can walk in the Grace.
We can walk together
to a Holy Place.

We walk with God together.
We walk with Him alone.
We take a sacred journey.
We are coming Home.

He gives His direction.
He gives the Clarion Call.
He will not let us stumble.
He will not let us fall.

We are protected,
filled with Love and Grace.
We are coming Home
to a Holy Place.

We journey together.
We are not alone.
God is always with us
on our journey Home.

Going Within

Going within,
there is no lack.
Only going outside
holds us back.

In His Presence,
we are safe,
We are released
from the grave.

A grave situation
where life is hard,
In the world
where is God?

Where is the love
in this place?
Where is His Presence?
Where is His Grace?

God is here
in this place.
His Light shines
in every face.

He heals our hearts.
He soothes our souls.
He takes our hand.
His Hand we hold.

In God's Kingdom
there are no swirls,
A place of love
not of this world.

We bring His Presence.
We shine His Light.
We bring His Love;
no more dark night.

We bring His Presence.
We bring our love,
not of this world,
but from above.

We awaken,
no empty dream.
We are Home
where we've always been.

In God's Kingdom,
there is no lack.
We have come Home.
We have come back.

A New Beginning

A new beginning,
A wake-up call;
His Presence
heals us all.

The world's plan,
all the pain,
now is washed
right down the drain.

We see the truth.
We hear God's Call.
We have answered,
no more to fall.

We have awakened,
no more to drift.
Home with God
without a script.

We are Home,
in God's Embrace.
We rest in Him.
We have God's Grace.

To Walk with God

To walk with God,
hand in hand.
To walk with God
on soft sand.

To walk with God,
a Holy Place.
To walk with God,
all pain erased.

All the scripts
that we have lived,
we now let go,
in Him we live.

We fly free,
our journey done.
We come home,
no more to roam.

We rest in God,
all pain erased.
We have come Home,
His Holy Place.

Songs of Joy

A wake-up call,
a gentle ring,
in His Presence
my heart sings.

Songs of joy,
songs of praise,
songs of love,
Amazing Grace.

We are Home,
in God's Embrace,
filled with love,
filled with grace.

This holy instant
salvation comes.
We awaken.
We are Home.

All the joy,
the sweet release.
We have God's Love.
We have God's Peace.

God Holds Your Hand

God holds your hand.
He lifts us all.
We have awakened.
We heard His Call.

His Love
enfolds us all.
With His Love
we cannot fall.

We fly free
to Heaven's Gate.
No more to wander.
No more to wait.

He is the Wind
beneath our wings.
The Bells of Heaven
now do ring.

They call us Home,
to hear His Call.
To awaken,
They call us all.

Only My Words

Only My Words
bring release.
All your struggles
now do cease.

All the burdens,
all the pain,
all released
with God's Holy Flame.

All the world,
the load we bear,
all the suffering,
all the snares.

Now do clear,
Our pain erased.
The truth now seen
in Christ's Holy Face.

The Face of Christ
now revealed.
The Light of God
no more concealed.

We are free
from the pain,
free from the world,
a world insane.

God's Holy Kingdom
now is here.
With new eyes
All is clear.

All are brothers.
All are One.
We rest in God,
His Holy Son.

Here's the Joy

Here's the Joy.
Here's the day.
We walk with God.
He shows the Way.

The Way, the Truth;
He is our Life.
We walk with Him
to Paradise.

We come Home;
our journey done.
One with God,
never alone.

The useless journey
now does end;
Heaven's Gate
around the bend.

We are free.
The past has passed.
All the joy;
we're Home at last.

His Words

I write my book.
I write His words.
The Voice for God
is now heard.

His Holy Presence
in every heart,
no one forsaken,
no one apart.

All can hear
His holy words.
In every heart;
His message heard.

We know in Silence.
We know today.
We know His Presence.
We know His Way.

God's Peace

In God's Embrace;
the dream erased.
A holy presence,
A holy place.

God is present.
God is here.
The clouds are gone.
All is clear.

There is no haze,
just bright sunshine;
a holy place
beyond space and time.

The door now open,
with eyes to see.
The Light now shines.
We are now free.

Free from the world,
the world released.
We have God's Love.
We have God's Peace.

Always Here

You are the sunshine.
There is no haze.
You are the Light;
just sunny days.

Our light hidden,
in the pain,
in the sadness,
in the rain.

Empty words,
just blaa, blaa, blaa,
all have hidden
who we are.

Time to let go;
we've paid our dues.
Time to let go
of singing the blues.

From the sadness,
from the pain;
We are reborn.
We are now sane.

The Light of God
within us all;
We open our eyes.
We hear His Call.

God is present,
always here.
We awaken.
All is clear.

Freedom's Gift,
it is not far.
Always here,
it's who we are.

Every Step

Every step,
every choice,
All is given
with God's Voice.

The Voice for God,
all is clear.
His Holy Presence,
always here.

He shows the Way,
the Truth, the Life.
His Holy Presence
heals all strife.

We are blessed;
held in His Arms.
God is with us.
We hear His Psalms.

We know His Presence,
His Holy Voice.
We feel His Love.
We've made the choice.

We now listen.
He shows the Way.
Always with us,
Here to stay.

God is Present

All the buildings,
all the land,
earthly mansions,
like shifting sands.

All that's present,
all that's real,
The love inside us
for us to feel.

To know God's Presence.
To know His Love.
A gift from Heaven,
from above.

No more seeking.
We are now found.
We stand with God
on Holy Ground.

To Rest

We come to God
with empty hands.
We hear His Voice.
We know His Plan.

His direction.
He calls us home.
The wayward sheep
no more do roam.

We let go
of our ideas.
Now His Voice
is so clear.

We sit, we rest
in God's Embrace.
We are now Home,
a Holy Place.

In our hearts
His Kingdom rests.
We are God's Kingdom.
We are so blessed.

We Stand

We bring peace
to all the land.
One with God,
with Him we stand.

All the struggles,
all the wars,
everything
that we abhor.

We release.
We now let go.
His Holy Presence
now does show.

No longer hidden,
we are now free.
In His Presence
we now can be.

We see the truth
beyond the lies,
no longer hidden,
no more disguised.

We have God's Peace.
We sing His Song.
We awaken.
A new world is born.

In His Hands

We trust His Plan.
With God we stand.
Our salvation
in His Hands.

All the struggles,
all the war,
now are silenced.
They are no more.

We are given
a new start.
We stand together,
no more apart.

We are woven;
His Cloth Divine.
The Light of God
now does shine.

Who Reigns?

Who reigns
the land of Ukraine?
The Presence of God
or a man insane?

His Love is here.
He holds our hand.
He heals all sadness.
He blesses the land.

Do we listen?
Do we hear His Call?
Or do we watch?
Or do we fall?

His Holy Presence,
His Love, His Grace,
all around us,
in every place.

We have a fork
in the road.
What will we choose?
What will unfold?

We can rise.
We can pray.
We sing His Song.
We start today.

We can awaken,
open our eyes,
see the truth
beneath the lies.

The call for love,
The call for peace,
The call for help,
God's sweet release.

His Light

All plans
in God's Hands;
He knows the Way,
the Way so grand.

The Guiding Light
within us all
knows the truth
beyond the wall.

Lifetimes hidden,
only a spark,
in the clouds,
in the dark.

Beyond the veil,
beyond the dream,
His Holy Kingdom
now is seen.

A Revelation
for us all,
to awaken,
to hear His Call.

He calls His flock.
He calls us Home.
We are with God,
no more alone.

The Firm Foundation of God

Where is our foundation? Who is our Foundation? Is it the world? Or is it God?

Like the Prodigal Son, we have wandered. We have roamed. God is our GPS. He calls us Home.

We have forgotten Who we are--the Holy Sons of a Loving Father, His Children. We were created by Love, as Love.

Now is the time to awaken.

There is a beautiful lesson in "A Course in Miracles" entitled "Father, I will but to remember You" (W.p2-231.) Now is the time to remember--to remember God and know His Holy Presence—the same Holy Presence in every heart. Now is the time to live our lives with kindness, forgiveness, mercy. Now is the time to live lives filled with the Love of God, for, in truth, we are filled with the Love of God.

Everything else is a nightmare, a dream. None of it is part of the Kingdom of God, a Kingdom filled only with His Love.

We are at a choice point, a tipping point for humanity. What do we choose—God or mammon? Only one choice brings kindness. Only one choice brings love. Now is the time for the healing, the awakening of humanity. Now is the time to come Home.

His Foundation

His Foundation,
always there,
Ever-present,
always here.

We have wandered.
We lost our way.
Yet He is with us,
here to stay.

A lonely road,
with travail,
A useless journey,
an empty trail.

A lonely road,
far from home.
We have wandered.
We have roamed.

He calls His sheep.
He calls His flock.
Our Foundation,
He is our Rock.

On His Ocean
we now sail,
no more trials,
no empty trail.

With His Love
we are free.
We can rest.
We can be.

In His Arms,
in His Embrace,
We have love.
We have Grace.

His Presence
now is clear,
In every heart,
everywhere.

The wayward sheep
now come Home.
No more to wander.
No more to roam.

We know His Love,
His Shining Face.
In every heart
Amazing Grace.

On Angels' Wings

We go
through Heaven's Door.
Home at last.
We wait no more.

One with God,
with Him we stand.
Illusions vanish,
just shifting sands.

His Holy Kingdom
beyond the dream.
No longer hidden.
It is now seen.

The joy, the grace,
beyond the Gate.
No more to wander.
No more to wait.

We fly Home.
Freedom's Bell now rings.
We fly Home
on angels' wings.

The Gift of Renewal

I heard a beep, letting me know the battery on my Wi-Fi hotspot was fully charged. God is our Battery, our Source. We shine His Light when we remember our connection with Him. Just as a lamp needs a connection to a battery or to an electrical outlet, we need our connection to our Source for the Light of God to shine through us. I thought of the Bible passage, "I am the vine, you are the branches." (John 15:5) We are recharged by being in the Silence, being in the Holy Presence of God. Our rest brings renewal.

Just as a battery is renewed, we are renewed by spending time with God. This time with Him is holy, sacred. It is time apart from the world. It is time with God, a time of healing, a time of renewal.

God's Holy Place

Above the battleground,
Home we fly.
We leave the earth
and touch the sky.

All the wars,
fought for naught,
All the suffering
we have wrought.

An unholy instant,
a madman's dream;
gone at last;
We are redeemed.

The nightmare gone.
We are now free.
With new eyes
We can now see.

The call for love
beyond the hate;
A new door opens,
Heaven's Gate.

We are now free,
no more to dream.
One with God;
We are redeemed.

We have come Home,
God's Holy Place.
All the joy,
Amazing Grace.

To Hear His Words

To hear His Words,
To sing His Song,
To share His Words,
To sing along.

We join together,
hand in hand,
God's Holy Chorus,
God's Joyous Band.

We are Home,
a holy place.
We sing His Song.
We know His Grace.

All together;
All are One.
The journey over,
The journey done.

We are Home;
now free at last.
The past now over;
The past has passed.

The long, hard journey,
the wandering roads,
now has ended;
new life unfolds.

Our life with God;
We are now One;
the useless journey
over and done.

With God We Stand

Letting go
of the world,
its peaks and valleys,
all the swirls.

We fly untethered.
We fly free.
One with God;
we can now see.

All the joy
is now known.
His Holy Presence;
all now shown.

His Holy Kingdom,
His Shining Light,
now is present,
now in sight.

A new day dawns.
His Kingdom here,
seen with open eyes,
seen everywhere.

All the shadows
now disappear.
The Love of God
seen everywhere.

In the world
beneath the sky,
We now see clearly,
with new eyes.

The call for love
to heal the pain.
He does answer,
a sweet refrain.

We join His Chorus.
We sing His Song.
A new world
is now born.

We awaken.
We share His Gift.
We have come Home,
no more to drift.

We are safe.
He holds our hand.
We are Home.
With God we stand.

On God Alone

On God alone,
salvation rests.
In His Arms,
we are so blessed.

Other voices,
other words,
now are silenced,
no longer heard.

In quiet words,
He speaks to us.
We hear, we listen,
in God, we trust.

We trust in Him,
in Him alone,
with such joy,
we have come Home.

The Graves of My Parents

The graves of my parents,
They've never been there, and
they've always been there.

Here, now, present, alive.
One with God,
One with me,
One with all humanity.

Their souls present.
Their gifts received.
Their love now given
and received.

A holy encounter,
One with God.
A new beginning
without end.

A Simple Journey

A simple journey;
a direct flight home.
All aboard;
no more to roam.

We now board
the freedom train.
Gone now
all the world's pain.

A new voyage;
His joy so clear.
We release
what we've held dear.

All the suffering,
all the pain,
all the world,
its sad refrain.

A new life given,
the joy, the grace.
Our life in God,
a holy place.

We release
the world, the pain.
No more singing
its sad refrain.

Our hearts now open.
Our souls fly free.
We awaken.
We can now see.

His Holy Presence,
His Holy Light,
heals our hearts,
undoes our fright.

One with God;
all is so clear.
No one absent.
All are here.

All aboard
the freedom train;
the Love of God
heals the world's pain.

All God's Children,
every daughter and son,
all together;
all are One.

One with God;
our journey done.
We have arrived.
We are now Home.

One with God;
we are so blessed.
We are Home;
in God we rest.

His Holy Kingdom;
all so clear;
His Holy Presence
always here.

His Holy Kingdom;
all so clear;
His Holy Presence
everywhere.

All Revealed

All revealed;
the truth now clear.
Illusions vanish
and disappear.

With open hearts,
with open eyes,
all is clear
with no disguise.

We can now see.
We can feel.
The dawning light,
all that is real.

A holy place,
the dawning light,
The Love of God
is now in sight.

The peace, the love;
a holy place.
We have come Home;
Amazing Grace.

The Return

Where do we turn?

In which direction do we go?

Who is our Guide? Do we follow the path of kindness, of love, of peace, or do we choose a different direction, a different way?

The Way of God is holy. The Way of God is kind.

We have taken detours, taken long and winding roads. We have been on an arduous journey.

Now is the time to rest, to rest in the Embrace of God.

He makes straight our paths--the Pathway Home to God.

We have wandered. We have roamed.

Now is the time for a new direction—a time to rest—to rest in the Presence of God.

In truth, we are always in His Presence. In truth, we are always in His Embrace. In His Arms we rest.

Our journey Home is a journey without distance. It is a lifting of the veil.

It is an awakening. It is the gift of freedom.

It is the Gift of Love.

One

His Loving Presence,
His comforting words,
in quiet sunlight
now are heard.

Always with us,
always there,
His Holy Presence,
His loving care.

We have waited,
felt the pain,
but our prayers
were not in vain.

Our voices heard,
His Answer here;
His Holy Presence,
all is clear.

In the shadows,
in the dark,
the Light of God
gives us His Spark.

A ray of sunshine,
shining bright,
fills us all
with His Light.

A ray of sunshine,
in us all.
We are awake.
We hear His Call.

One with God.
We sing His Song.
His Holy Chorus;
Our voices strong.

We join together.
We join His Band.
One with God,
hand in hand.

On the Water

He makes the plans.
He guides the ship.
His wayward sheep
no more to drift.

On the water
we set sail.
One with God,
we cannot fail.

We travel on,
with faith alone.
We take the journey,
the journey Home.

A peaceful journey,
a gentle trail.
We rest in God
as we set sail.

There is no distance.
We all are One.
God's Holy Child,
God's Holy Son.

Letting Go

Letting go;
no words to say.
All the world
fades away.

Illusions gone,
never real.
The Love of God
we now do feel.

We fly free.
We fly high.
We soar above
the earth and sky.

We have come Home.
We find our rest.
We are at peace.
We are so blessed.

In holy silence,
in quiet words,
the Voice for God
is now heard.

His Message given.
We hear His Word.
Our hearts open.
His Message heard.

We join together.
We join as One.
We live in God,
His Holy Son.

Heaven's Door

Heaven's Door,
now revealed.
Heaven's Gate,
no more concealed.

His Shining Light,
His Joy, His Grace,
all now seen,
a Holy Place.

The Light of God
shines away
all the sadness,
every fray.

Our hearts open.
We can now see.
We can rest.
We are free.

In His Arms,
God above,
above the world,
We know His Love.

Only One

Only One;
One Soul.
All is One.
We are now whole.

We leave the theater,
an empty screen.
We awaken;
no more to dream.

We let go.
We find our rest.
One with God,
His bequest.

Illusions vanish,
all now clear.
Tears of joy,
our Home is here.

No other,
Only One.
God's Holy Child,
God's Holy Son.

Freedom

All the pain,
washed away.
All the sadness,
gone today.

A new beginning,
a new life.
Freedom dawns,
no more strife.

On the shore,
in the waves
we let go,
no longer slaves.

Forgiveness given;
all released.
We have joy.
We have peace.

Our hearts open.
We now see.
A new beginning,
We are free.

God's Blessing

We follow His footsteps.
He shows us the way.
He blazes the trail.
We cannot go astray.

All is clear;
the sun shines bright.
We see the truth.
We see the Light.

The Light of God;
our way now clear.
We feel His Love.
He holds us dear.

In His Arms,
in God's Embrace,
We know love.
We have grace.

A Father's Blessing
to us all;
We awaken.
We hear God's Call.

He calls us Home,
to Heaven's Gate,
no more to wander,
no more to wait.

Tears of joy;
a holy place.
We have come Home;
Amazing Grace.

A New Life

A new life
begins today.
All the sadness
has gone away.

All the suffering,
all the lies,
hidden by
a thin disguise.

A false veneer,
the ego's lies.
We awaken.
We are now wise.

All the wisdom,
born from pain.
We now waken.
We are now sane.

We now see
beyond the lies,
what was hidden
and disguised.

The priceless gifts
in everyone;
all God's Daughters,
all God's Sons.

The Call for love,
the beauty seen.
Now revealed
beyond the dream.

A glorious sunrise;
the Light in all.
As it was
before the fall.

We now see.
We now know,
the life, the joy,
where we go.

We go to God.
We travel on.
All our suffering
now is gone.

We are free.
We are strong.
We join together.
We sing along.

No lonely road,
no empty trail,
no more to suffer,
no more travail.

We have joy.
We have grace.
We are free;
a holy place.

The Presence

The Presence of God,
without a sound,
in the quiet,
all around.

In the stillness,
we are reborn.
The Light of God
now does dawn.

This holy instant,
all pain erased.
The world disappears,
without a trace.

This holy instant,
all is seen,
God's Holy Kingdom,
beyond the dream.

The Light of God,
all around,
now is present,
now is found.

This holy instant,
no time or place.
We know Love,
Amazing Grace.

My Garden

My garden grows
by the cove,
filled with joy,
filled with love.

A quiet place,
the colors bright,
God is present.
We see His Light.

All the flowers,
all the trees,
swaying gently
in the breeze.

We see the waves,
the ocean blue,
God's Holy Presence,
We know what's true.

A doorway opens.
A new space dawns.
We awaken.
We are reborn.

Born in love,
born in grace.
In His Presence,
a holy place.

We are God's garden,
His flowers, His seed.
We now blossom.
We are free.

The clouds now vanish;
they disappear.
The veil is lifted.
All is clear.

We see the truth,
beyond the lies,
what was hidden,
what was disguised.

The beauty seen,
in everyone.
We are God's garden,
every daughter and son.

Every Child

Every child
is an indigo child,
if we have eyes to see.

Every child
is an indigo child,
when we see who they can be.

All are gifts,
all are love.
Gifts from Heaven,
from above.

No one special,
all are One,
all God's Children,
every daughter and son.

The gifts of God
fill us all.
We are His Kingdom.
We hear His Call.

With open eyes,
and open hearts,
we are together,
not apart.

His gifts we share.
We see, we know.

His Holy Light
now does show.

All aglow,
shining bright.
We see the sun.
We see the light.

All aglow,
shining bright.
We are God's Son,
filled with His Light.

No one special,
or alone.
We join together.
We have come Home.

No one special.
We join as One.
We are His Child,
His Holy Son.

Not Here

Not here,
or over there.
One with God;
all is clear.

The empty vessel,
the paper cup.
We let go.
We've had enough.

We see clearly,
with new eyes;
to the dream-world
we give our good-byes.

He fills us up.
He fills us all.
We know His Love.
We now stand tall.

We now arise;
a new day dawns.
We awaken.
We are reborn.

We have come Home.
We know His Love.
We have His peace,
like the turtle doves.

The God of Love

The God of Love
won't let you fall.
The God of Love
hears your call.

A call for love,
a call for peace,
a call for freedom
and release.

A new day dawns;
the sweet sunrise.
We awaken
and open our eyes.

We see the beauty
in us all.
We have His gifts.
He hears our call.

Our call for love,
answered true.
A new beginning;
we start anew.

All forgiven,
all pain erased,
all in order,
all in place.

His Hand on all.
His Love abounds.
We once were lost,
and now we're found.

We have arrived;
the journey ends.
We are with
our Holy Friend.

We have joy.
We have peace.
The past now gone,
the past released.

A new beginning.
A brand-new day.
We have come Home.
We found our way.

All Aboard

We board the Freedom Train.
Gone is the world and all its pain.

We see the light of distant stars.
Now we remember Who we are.

We come Home,
our sweet return.
We awaken,
our lessons learned.

The Light of God,
from Heaven above.
We feel the joy.
We feel the love.

There's the Freedom

There's the freedom.
We now let go.
God's Holy Presence
now does show.

We let go
of our plans.
Illusions vanish,
like shifting sands.

We know His plan.
He guides us all.
We hear His Voice.
We hear His Call.

We rest in God,
in His Embrace.
We have come Home,
filled with God's Grace.

Angels here,
all around.
They touch our hearts
with quiet sounds.

Bringing joy
and happiness.
They give our hearts
a place to rest.

We rest in God,
no more alone.
We have arrived.
We have come Home.

In the Quiet

Beyond vibration,
beyond sound;
God's Holy Kingdom,
all around.

There is no earth.
There is no sky.
There is no you.
There is no I.

Only God,
His Joy, His Light.
All is One.
All is bright.

In quiet stillness,
without a sound;
God's Holy Presence,
all around.

In the quiet;
no sound can be.
We are Home.
We are free.

In Holy Silence;
the world released.
We are Home.
We are at peace.

We remember,
before the fall.
Illusions vanish;
God's Silent Call.

He Calls us Home,
unto His Light,
with His Love,
with His Sight.

Our sight restored;
we are at peace.
Illusions vanish;
all released.

One with God,
One with all,
as it was
before the fall.

We rise together.
We rise as One.
We are Home,
the journey done.

We awaken.
We join as One.
One with God.
We are His Son.

In the quiet;
God is found.
His Holy Kingdom,
all around.

In Quiet Words

In the quiet,
God's Answer shows.
Like a river
it does flow.

In quiet words
and open hearts,
with His Love
a new start.

All is clear;
the sun shines bright,
no more clouds,
no dark night,

All the joy,
all the grace;
we have come
to a new place.

We are Home,
in God's Embrace.
One with God,
filled with His Grace.

Resting with God

Rest with God.
Walk with Me.
There is an answer
you cannot see.

All is clear.
All is known.
With My Hand
all is shown.

In My time,
My Holy Way,
all God's blessings
here today.

We receive
the grace, the peace,
all the suffering
we release.

We wait, we listen.
We hear His Song.
We raise our voices,
our voices strong.

All the clouds,
gone today.
Clear skies
are here to stay.

My Ticket Home

My ticket home,
the fare all paid.
I travel on,
no more afraid.

Releasing all
the ties that bind.
The ancient thread
does unwind.

I let go
and release;
I have come Home.
I have God's Peace.

All the drama,
all the pain,
the useless journey,
the sad refrain.

All the tears
I have shed,
all the fears,
all the dread.

I release,
and I let go.
God is here.
The Light does show.

All the sadness,
all the pain,
the useless journey
of a world insane.

Now I see,
now I know.
I awaken,
and I let go.

A new beginning,
a new day born.
A new life
now does dawn.

The Call

Dream big,
dream small.
Or awaken,
not to dream at all.

All the stuff
of the earth,
the false gifts
with no worth.

All the glitter,
all the gold.
All the lies
that we've been told.

The false world,
all the stuff.
We awaken.
We've had enough.

We awaken.
We let go.
In His River
does our life flow.

One with God,
His Kingdom here.
All now seen.
All is clear.

A new world
awaits us all.
We come Home.
We hear God's Call.

God's Holy Kingdom
no more concealed.
The Love of God,
now revealed.

Our Home in God,
no dream at all.
A place of peace,
we hear the Call.

Angels Here

Angels here,
all around,
In the quiet,
they abound.

They guide us all,
night and day,
ever-present,
in all ways.

Always with us,
they hear our call.
They hear, they answer.
They love us all.

Bringing love,
bringing peace;
the old world vanishes,
our sweet release.

A new world born.
A new world seen.
We awaken,
no more to dream.

On angels' wings
we come home,
no more to wander,
no more to roam.

God's Holy Presence;
all is clear,
always with us,
always here.

In His Presence

I release.
I let go.
His Holy Presence
now does show.

All the burdens
I have borne,
now are lifted,
now are shorn.

The weight lifted
from my shoulders,
every load,
all the boulders.

My shoulders free
I now rest.
In His Presence,
I am blessed.

All the burdens,
all the weight,
all the sorrow,
all the hate.

The world's weight,
all the boulders,
now are gone
from my shoulders.

I fly free.
I see clear.
His Holy Presence
now is here.

Always with us,
through the pain,
through the sorrow,
in the rain.

The clouds now gone,
they disappear.
Only God
now is here.

One with God.
One with life,
free of burdens,
free of strife.

We do more
than just survive.
We awaken.
We now thrive.

We are Home,
free at last.
The old world gone
the past has passed.

We rest in
God's Holy Place,
filled with love
Amazing Grace.

In God's Kingdom

In God's Kingdom
no ties that bind,
from the earth's web
we do unwind.

We let go
and hear our hearts.
One with God,
no more apart.

Tears of joy,
tears of grace;
in everyone
we see God's Face.

God's direction
we have our parts.
We know the truth
that's in our hearts.

We now rest.
We now let go.
In God's River
our lives flow.

His direction;
He guides us all.
We cannot stumble.
We cannot fall.

He leads us Home.
We follow along.
A holy chorus,
We sing His Song.

Our Holy Friend

Above the battleground
we now stand,
bringing peace
to all the land.

All on earth,
all yet to come,
to every daughter,
to every son.

In everyone,
God's Face now seen,
bringing peace
from beyond the dream.

We awaken,
the veil released.
We have freedom.
We have peace.

A new beginning,
without end;
we walk with
our Holy Friend.

Hand in hand,
Heart to heart.
We join as One.
We have our part.

His Holy Kingdom,
all is clear,
ever-present,
always here.

In God's Presence

In His Presence,
there are no words.
In quiet sounds
God's Voice is heard.

We hear, we see,
the life around,
in the quiet,
without a sound.

In the Silence,
we are blessed,
a holy place
for us to rest.

We awaken,
now to see,
a quiet place
for us to be.

We hear, we listen,
to what's inside,
the holy place
where God resides.

All Around

I am the Answer.
I am the Way.
Hear My Voice,
listen today.

All the lies
that you've been told,
the world's way
of being bold.

All the lies
that you've been told,
all the lies
the world has sold.

A quiet answer,
no storms abound.
In quiet listening
God is found.

Always with us,
always here,
always present,
all now clear.

In the quiet,
we now see.
In His Presence,
here to be.

The quiet tears,
without a sound,
God is present,
all around.

A Sacred Place

A sacred place
for us to go.
A sacred place,
where God does show.

We have wandered.
We have roamed.
We have gone
far from our home.

To the mountains,
to the sea,
wondering
where God could be.

We have looked,
We have not seen
the only place
where God has been.

God is with us.
He does not hide,
ever-present,
deep inside.

In our hearts,
in our souls,
we see, we know.
We are whole.

He is with us,
always here,
never far,
always near.

We now know
Who we are,
bright as any
shining star.

God is with us,
always here,
always present,
all is clear.

God's Kingdom

Letting go
of the world,
its peaks and valleys,
all the swirls.

We fly untethered.
We fly free.
One with God,
We can now see.

All the joy
is now known.
His Holy Presence,
all now shown.

His Holy Kingdom,
His Holy Light,
now is present,
now in sight.

Here with God

Here with God,
with Him we stand,
bringing peace
to all the land.

In holy silence,
we now see.
We awaken.
We are free.

From the storms,
illusions borne,
We let go.
Illusions shorn.

Only God,
His Holy Hand,
bringing peace
to all the land.

In the quiet
we hear God's Voice.
We hear, we listen.
We make the choice.

We choose for God,
the Voice of Peace.
He gives His gifts,
our sweet release.

Seeing Clear

Seeing clear,
with new eyes,
seeing beyond
the world's disguise.

The truth revealed,
the unseen seen,
what lies beyond
an unholy dream.

All the world
fades away.
We can see,
see today.

Underneath
the world's disguise,
seeing beyond
the hate and lies.

All the love
we see anew,
with fresh eyes,
like morning dew.

Our innocence,
now reborn
all the blinders
now are shorn.

We let go;
we release.
We see anew.
We have God's Peace.

In each other,
seen with new eyes,
we see beyond
the world's disguise.

All the love,
always there.
All the joy
we now share.

We see anew;
a new day dawns.
We now wake.
We are reborn.

In God's Kingdom,
a holy place,
filled with love,
Amazing Grace.

The Garden

The Garden grows,
flowers bloom.
Returning Home,
very soon.

All in order,
in God's Hands,
as we fulfill
His Holy Plan.

The dream does end,
all crystal clear.
We come Home,
God's Kingdom here.

All the flowers
given away.
All the Love
here today.

Everything,
all crystal clear.
God is present,
always here.

Home Today

The world
goes away.
This holy instant,
gone today.

We have
gone astray.
We come
home today.

All released,
all undone,
freedom for
God's Holy Son.

The Christ in me,
born today.
The world has
gone away.

The Christ in all,
born today.
The world has
gone away.

No more are we
led astray.
We come
Home today.

My Light

My Light shows
for all to see.
With God's Love
we are now free.

No more clouds,
just sunny days,
no more darkness,
no more haze.

The Light so bright,
fills us all.
Deep inside us,
we stand tall.

We arise,
no more to dream,
filled with love,
we are redeemed.

All the love
beyond the sky,
fills us all,
fills you and I.

We return,
no more to roam,
no more to dream,
we have come Home.

Never Real

Illusions gone,
never there.
God is present,
everywhere.

The cloudy skies,
the anger and pain,
washed away
with the spring rain.

Never present,
never real,
We now see.
We now heal.

The movie ends,
the last film reel.
All the love
we now do feel.

Our hearts know,
now we see,
from the pain
we are now free.

It was
never real.
Only love
we now do feel.

We see and know
who we are,
the brightest light,
the brightest star.

Everyone,
everywhere,
all the love
we now share.

We come together.
We join as One.
We are God's Treasure,
His Holy Son.

Returning Home

Here in the Silence,
Here all around,
this quiet morning,
Here God is found.

The way now open
now we can see.
In God's Holy Kingdom
we are now free.

With every person,
in every heart,
we join together,
no one apart.

God's Holy Kingdom,
in every soul.
In His Holy Presence,
we are now whole.

We join together.
We join as One.
We are God's Treasure,
God's Holy Son.

Our journey completed,
over and done.
Through the Gates of Heaven,
we have come Home.

Here's the Miracle

Here's the miracle.
Here's the day,
in My time,
in My way.

The scheduled time
now arrives.
We awaken,
not just survive.

The scheduled time
now arrives.
We awaken,
now to thrive.

We live in God,
never alone,
One with all,
our holy Home.

All is present,
all is here,
God's Holy Light
shines everywhere.

The truth now seen.
All is known.
God's Love present.
God's Love shown.

We have joy.
We see God's Face,
in everyone,
filled with His Grace.

Filled with love,
filled with light,
filled with joy,
the Light so bright.

Touches all,
everyone,
All of God's Children,
every daughter and son.

Always Present

Always Present,
Always here.
Like a bell,
sounding clear.

Tides of joy
bringing peace,
filled with love,
our sweet release.

In the Silence,
in quiet times,
hear the bells,
hear the chimes.

In our innocence
we see the sun.
We join together.
We join as One.

One with God,
He holds our hands.
Solid Rock,
not shifting sands.

In each other,
in everyone,
the Face of Christ,
we see God's Son.

We join together,
hand in hand.
We bring aloha
to the land.

Love is Here

Love is here,
all around,
in the quiet,
without a sound.

Beyond time.
beyond space,
filled with love,
filled with grace.

In the stillness,
without a sound,
God is present,
all around.

In the joy,
the sky so bright,
filled with love,
God's Holy Light.

Everywhere,
all around,
God is present,
God is found.

He Carries Us Home

We come to God,
to God alone,
Always with us,
He carries us Home.

We return,
no more to wait.
We now go through
Heaven's Gate.

In the Silence,
filled with grace,
We come to
God's Holy Place.

In His Kingdom,
we return.
We are Home,
our lessons learned.

In God's Kingdom,
we now rest.
We are Home.
We are blessed.

In Everyone

We fly free.
We fly alone.
One with God,
We have come Home.

All the stories,
all the tales,
we now go
beyond the veils.

Filled with joy,
filled with light,
God's Holy Presence
now in sight.

We release.
We now let go.
There is no world.
The Light does show.

In us all,
in everyone,
in every child,
every daughter and son.

The Light of God
in us all.
We awaken.
We hear His Call.

We awaken,
our journey done.
We have arrived.
We are at Home.

With deep gratitude to
Marjorie Tyler, Sharon Lund, Sara Niccolls,
Jennifer Pryor, Helfried Zrzavy, Bill Van Nimwegen,
Joann Sjolander, and Margaret Ballonoff.